MEXICO: A Culture from Conquest

By Lorraine McCombs

Scott Foresman
is an imprint of

Glenview, Illinois • Boston, Massachusetts • Chandler, Arizona •
Upper Saddle River, New Jersey

Photographs

Every effort has been made to secure permission and provide appropriate credit for photographic material. The publisher deeply regrets any omission and pledges to correct errors called to its attention in subsequent editions.

Unless otherwise acknowledged, all photographs are the property of Pearson Education, Inc.

Photo locators denoted as follows: Top (T), Center (C), Bottom (B), Left (L), Right (R), Background (Bkgd)

Opener: (B) ©DK Images, (TC) ©Jack Hollingsworth/Corbis, (TR) ©The Granger Collection, NY, (TL) ©Scala/Art Resource, NY; **1** ©The Granger Collection, NY/©The Granger Collection, NY; **3** (B) ©DK Images, (TC) ©Jack Hollingsworth/Corbis, (TR) ©The Granger Collection, NY, (TL) ©Scala/Art Resource, NY; **4** (TL) ©Helene Rogers/Alamy Images, (Bkgd) ©DEA/G.DAGLI ORTI/Getty Images; **5** (T) ©Photofrenetic/Alamy Images; **6** Bibllioteca Medicea Laurenziana, Florence/©DK Images; **7** ©Gianni Dagli Orti/Corbis; **8** ©Bettmann/Corbis; **9** ©Erich Lessing/Art Resource, NY; **10** ©David Ashby/©DK Images; **11** ©Beuzon, J. L. (fl.1933)/Private Collection/Archives Charmet/Bridgeman Art Library; **12** ©The Granger Collection, NY/©The Granger Collection, NY; **13** ©dk/Alamy Images; **14** Spanish School, (16th century)/Private Collection/Bridgeman Art Library; **15** (Inset) ©Franz-Marc Frei/Corbis, (Bkgd) ©Kim Steele/Getty Images.

ISBN 13: 978-0-328-47300-7
ISBN 10: 0-328-47300-6

5 6 7 8 9 10 V010 13 12

Before Spain

Many different groups of people lived in ancient Mexico. The Aztecs were one of the most powerful of these groups.

The Aztecs came to Mexico from the north. They named themselves *Mexicas* after the land. They built a grand city and named it Tenochtitlan. This city would one day become the site of Mexico City, which is now the capital of Mexico.

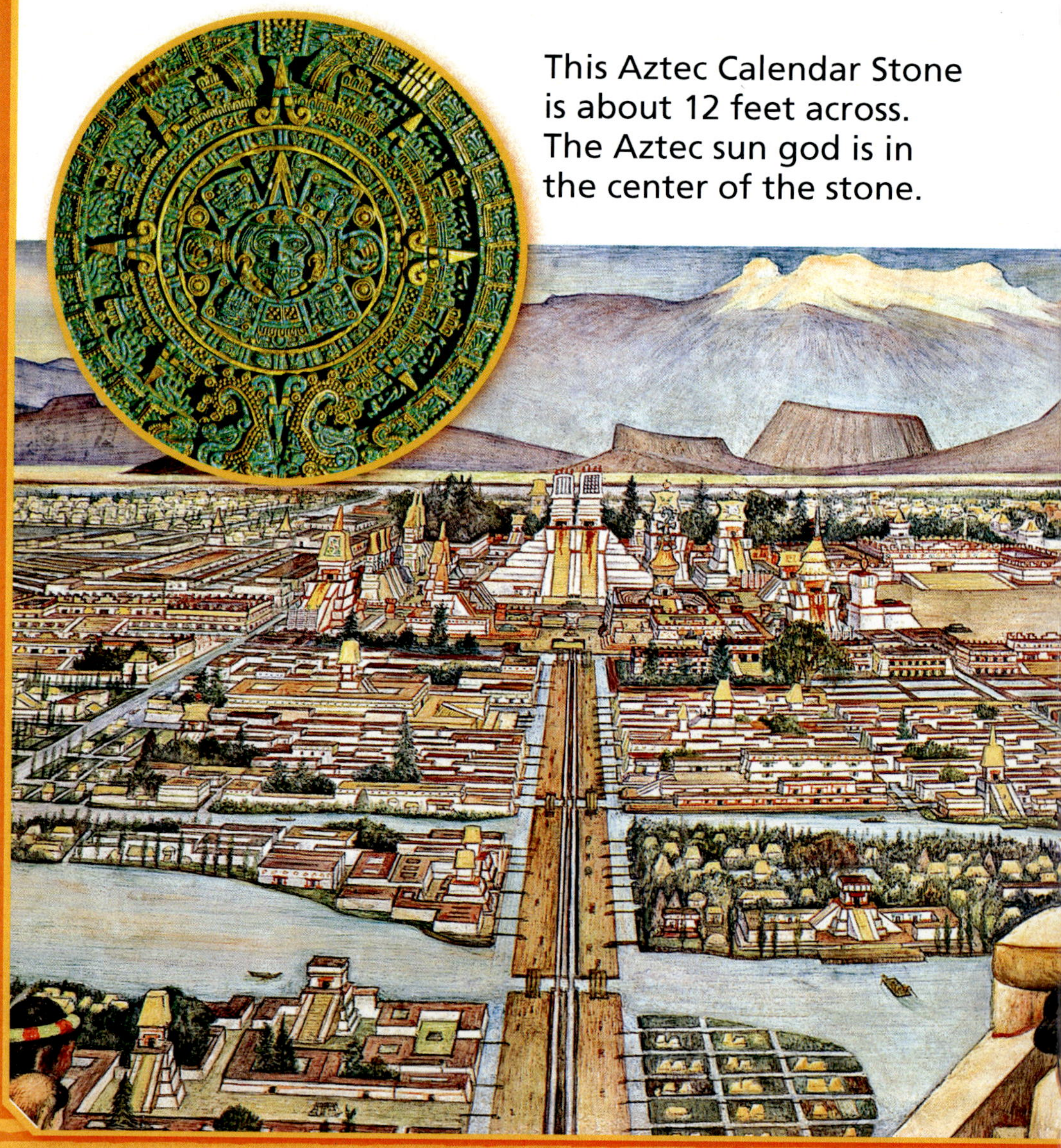

This Aztec Calendar Stone is about 12 feet across. The Aztec sun god is in the center of the stone.

The Aztecs were a fierce people, and war was important to them. Time after time, they defeated armies from neighbors who wanted to take over their land.

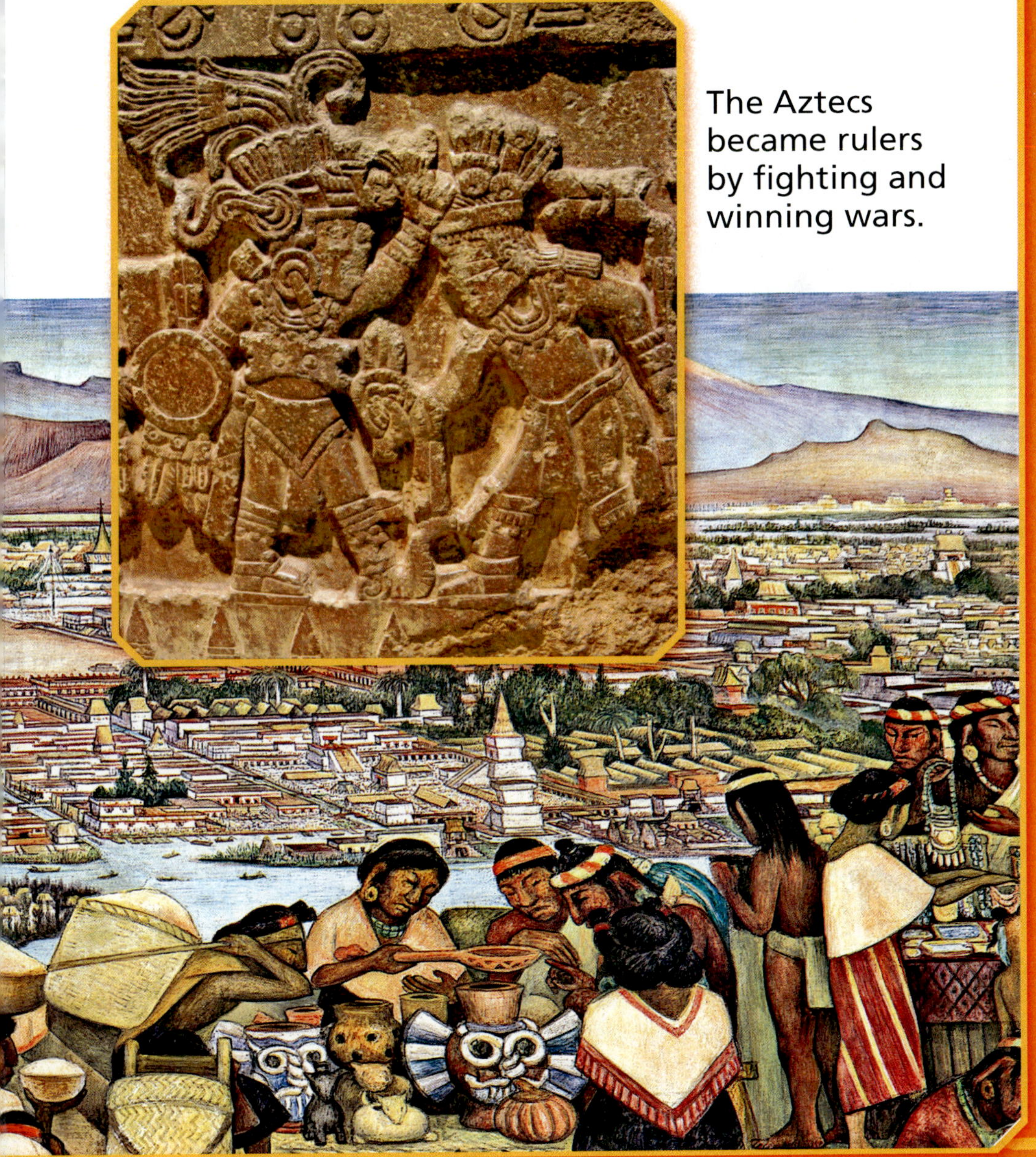

The Aztecs became rulers by fighting and winning wars.

The Aztecs had a very organized **society**. There were **nobles** and priests, who had most of the power. There were craftspeople, doctors, and teachers. Most people were farmers and laborers.

Peasants and slaves worked the land owned by the nobles. Most slaves were people who had been captured in a war. Some of them were slaves because they owed money or committed a crime.

Education was important to the Aztecs. Boys and girls first learned from their parents. Boys then went to school, but most girls stayed home. All children learned about the **traditions** of their society, including the special dances that were done to tell stories about brave warriors.

The Aztecs had many enemies and went to war often. People did not like the way the Aztecs treated them. These same people would one day help a more powerful enemy defeat the Aztecs.

The Spanish Arrive

In 1492 Christopher Columbus sailed from Spain hoping to find a new way to India. Instead, he found lands that Europeans called the New World.

Columbus returned to Spain with stories of treasure from this New World. Soon, more **explorers** came from Europe, looking for gold and other treasures.

Native people thought the explorers were very strange. Their skin was pale, and they spoke words the natives couldn't understand. They wore armor, rode horses, and carried guns. Some of the native people even thought they were gods.

The explorers said the new land belonged to Spain. But the idea that Spain owned their land didn't make sense to the native people.

The natives didn't like these new people, and they didn't like what was happening. They fought with the Spaniards to protect their cities, traditions, and way of life.

However, the native people were no match for Spanish guns, horses, and armies. In time, Spaniards **conquered** groups of native people in North and South America. They started **colonies** and brought in their own laws, language, and religion.

Spain established colonies in North and South America in the areas highlighted in pink.

The native people had their own religion, which was very different from the Spaniards' religion. Most Spaniards ignored the native culture and tried to destroy the natives' traditions. In some places this worked. In others it did not.

Mexico Today

Modern Mexico has its own culture, just as the native people and the Spaniards did long ago. Mexican culture today is a blend of both native and Spanish traditions.

Glossary

colonies *n.* settlements in new lands

conquered *v.* won a war with an enemy

explorers *n.* travelers who discover new lands or information

native *adj.* born in a certain place or country

nobles *n.* high-ranking people or families

peasants *n.* poor farmers that live and work a piece of land for the landowner

society *n.* people who live together in a group or culture

traditions *n.* beliefs and customs that are handed down